THE NBA BOOK OF BIG AND LITTLE

JAMES PRELLER

SCHOLASTIC INC.

NEW YORK   TORONTO   LONDON   AUCKLAND   SYDNEY

FOR ALL THE LITTLE GUYS
WITH BIG DREAMS
—J.P.

Photo Credits
Front Cover (legs), 3 (Bryant), 7, 23, 28, 29, Back Cover (Longley):
NBA/Andrew D. Bernstein. **Front Cover (Hardaway), 3 (Smits):** NBA/Ron
Hoskins. **Back Cover (Stoudamire):** NBA/Steven Freeman. **2:** NBA/Gregg
Forwerck. **3 (Marbury), 24:** NBA/Dave Sherman. **9:** NBA/Tim O'Dell.
10, 27: NBA/Glenn James. **11, 31:** NBA/Louis Capozzola.
12, 13: PhotoDisc, Inc. **16, 20:** NBA/Scott Cunningham. **17:** NBA/Jerry
Wachter. **18, 25:** NBA/Nathaniel S. Butler. **19:** NBA/Christopher J. Relke.
21: NBA/Bill Baptist. **22, 30:** NBA/Patrick Murphy-Racey.
26: NBA/Rocky Widner. **32:** NBA/Andy King.

ISBN 0-590-37756-6

© 1998 by NBA Properties, Inc.
All rights reserved. Published by Scholastic Inc.

12 11 10 9 8 7 6 5 4 3 2 1   8 9/9 0 1 2 3/0

Printed in the U.S.A.
First Scholastic printing, February 1998
Book design: Michael Malone

MUGGSY BOGUES
5'3"

STEPHON MARBURY
6'1"

RIK SMITS
7'4"

Pacers
45

LAKERS
8

TIMBERWOLVES
3

KOBE BRYANT
6'6"

7'6"

7'

6'6"

6'

5'6"

5'

4'6"

4'

3'6"

3'

2'6"

2'

1'6"

1'

The NBA includes 29 teams, starring
the best basketball players on the planet.

BOSTON CELTICS

MIAMI HEAT

NEW JERSEY NETS

NEW YORK KNICKS

ATLANTA HAWKS

CHARLOTTE HORNETS

CHICAGO BULLS

CLEVELAND CAVALIERS

DALLAS MAVERICKS

DENVER NUGGETS

HOUSTON ROCKETS

MINNESOTA TIMBERWOLVES

GOLDEN STATE WARRIORS

LOS ANGELES CLIPPERS

LOS ANGELES LAKERS

PHOENIX SUNS

ORLANDO MAGIC

PHILADELPHIA 76ERS

WASHINGTON WIZARDS

DETROIT PISTONS

INDIANA PACERS

MILWAUKEE BUCKS

TORONTO RAPTORS

SAN ANTONIO SPURS

UTAH JAZZ

VANCOUVER GRIZZLIES

PORTLAND TRAIL BLAZERS

SACRAMENTO KINGS

SEATTLE SONICS

Some are
BIG.

SHAQUILLE O'NEAL IS SEVEN FEET, ONE INCH TALL.
HE WEIGHS 301 POUNDS.

Some are little.

AT ONLY FIVE FEET, THREE INCHES, MUGGSY BOGUES IS THE SMALLEST PLAYER IN NBA HISTORY.

TALL
PLAYERS

can be
as big as...

**SHAWN BRADLEY IS ONE OF THE
TALLEST PLAYERS IN THE NBA. HE
IS SEVEN FEET, SIX INCHES.**

9
basketballs!

or...

14
piggy banks!

35
chocolate
chip cookies!

6
televisions!

30
tennis balls!

10
toy monsters!

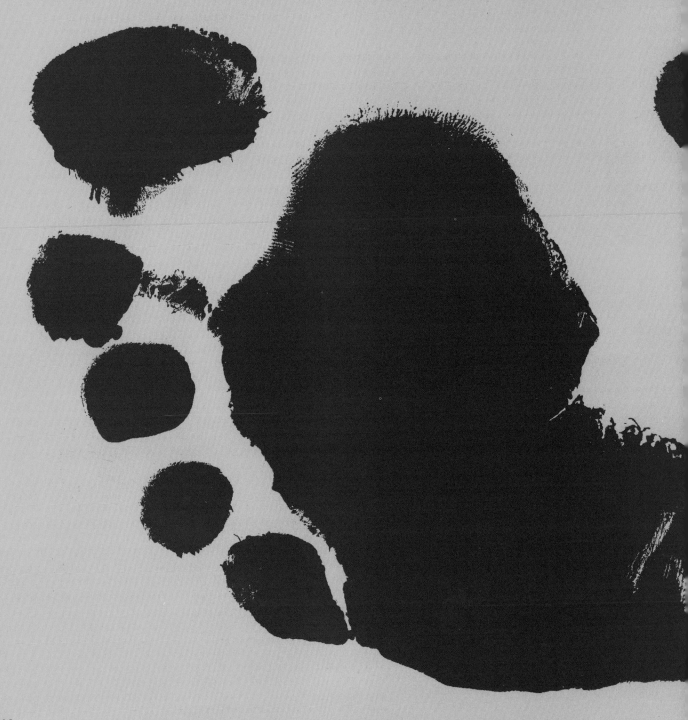

Here's what a footprint made by
Shaquille O'Neal might look like.
His sneakers are fifteen and
a half inches long.

That's big!

It's fun to be tall!

▲GHEORGHE MURESAN TOWERS OVER A CROWD OF YOUNG FANS.

◀DIKEMBE MUTOMBO

Tall players are
strong and powerful.
They can reach

HIGH!

◀ PATRICK EWING AND DIKEMBE MUTOMBO

BRYANT "BIG COUNTRY" REEVES ▶

Tall players can
DUNK
the basketball!

▲ HAKEEM "THE DREAM" OLAJUWON

◄ GREG OSTERTAG

With all those big guys around, it's not easy being a small player in the NBA.

▲ JOHN WALLACE BLOCKS A SHOT BY MUGGSY BOGUES.

MITCH RICHMOND ▶

But you don't have to be big to do great things.

▲ NICK "THE QUICK" VAN EXEL

◄ STEPHON MARBURY USES HIS SPEED TO BEAT BIGGER, STRONGER PLAYERS.

Small players are fast and quick.

TYUS EDNEY

Small players have to try harder.

DAMON STOUDAMIRE

JOHN STOCKTON

Small
players
can
jump
high...

and jam, too!

ONLY FIVE FEET, SEVEN INCHES, SPUD WEBB SHOCKED THE WORLD WHEN HE WON THE NESTLÉ CRUNCH SLAM DUNK CHAMPIONSHIP. LET'S HEAR IT FOR THE LITTLE GUYS! ▶

jump

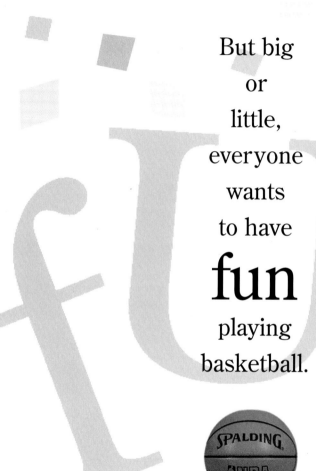

But big
or
little,
everyone
wants
to have
fun
playing
basketball.

◀ **MUGGSY BOGUES CELEBRATES WITH TEAMMATE VLADE DIVAC.**

So get out there and...
have a ball!